# THE POWER TO SAY

# *Yes*

Christine Assouad

To join The **Power to Say Yes** community, use this QR code

To my daughters, **Thea** & **Sara**

May you always live a happy, meaningful life on your own terms!

And I will be here, every step of the way ☺

# TABLE OF CONTENTS

# INTRODUCTION

# WHY THIS BOOK EXISTS

I used to think that being a woman didn't make any difference in how we built our careers.

When I was younger, I approached life and business with the mindset that everything was equal. Same opportunities, same rules. If you worked hard, stayed focused, and made smart decisions, success would follow, gender didn't matter. I started my first business at 22, and I never saw myself as limited by being a woman. If anything, I thought ignoring the "differences" was the best way to stay ahead.

## Then life happened.

I became a mom to two amazing daughters. I went through a divorce. I built more businesses. And, most importantly, I had the privilege of working with over 3,700 women. Through those one-on-one conversations, workshops, coaching sessions, and shared moments of doubt and clarity, I started to see something I had missed before.

**There is a difference.**

Not in talent, ambition, or potential; but in the layers of life we carry, in the choices we have to make, and in the invisible forces that shape our paths.

We are not just professionals. We are mothers, daughters, partners, caregivers, friends. We are constantly navigating between personal fulfillment and professional goals. And that blend, while messy at times, is also what gives us our unique power.
This book is my way of putting everything I've learned into something useful and hopeful. It's for every woman who has asked herself:

- *Can I be ambitious and still want a slow-paced life?*
- *What if I don't want to climb the ladder; but I still want to feel successful?*
- *Why do I feel so guilty for wanting more (or less)?*
- *How do I stop comparing my journey to everyone else's?*

If you've asked yourself any of these, **you're not alone.** And more importantly; **you're not stuck.** You have choices. Lots of them.

What I've seen over and over is that women often don't realize how many options they actually have. Sometimes we get trapped in guilt. Sometimes in comparison. Sometimes in pressure; pressure to prove something, to keep up, to do it all perfectly, to feel good enough. And sometimes we just don't have the right tools, support, or perspective to see that there are different paths to happiness and meaning.

What's exciting about being a woman today is that we're not limited to one formula for success. We don't have to follow anyone's script. We can design lives that fit us; not the other way around.

But to do that, we need to understand the landscape. We need to be aware of the systems, expectations, and trade-offs that influence our choices; and then make conscious, empowered decisions based on what matters to us.

This book is structured in three parts, and each part is designed to help you move from awareness to action:

- **Part I:** Understanding the Landscape. We'll explore how and why career decisions look different for women, what options exist, and what trade-offs come with each path. No judgment. Just clarity.
- **Part II:** Designing Your Life. Once you've mapped your options, it's time to decide what you want; and build your career and life around it, not the other way around.
- **Part III:** Living It Out. It's not enough to know what you want. You'll need boundaries, time and energy strategies, and real support systems to stay on track.

My hope is that this book becomes your personal guide. A reminder that you don't have to choose between joy and success. A toolkit to help you create a life that feels like yours, not someone else's version of it.

There's no single right answer here. No perfect balance. Just a series of decisions that align with your values, your season of life, and your vision of meaning. Whether you're building a business, growing your career, raising a family, taking a break, or pivoting entirely; you have **the power to say yes** to what truly matters.

So let's begin. Not with pressure or perfection; but with

## possibility.

**Christine Assouad** is a serial entrepreneur, mentor, and board advisor with over 28 years of experience, particularly in the Food & Beverage sector. At just 22, she brought **Dunkin' Donuts** to Lebanon, later expanding to over 40 locations and supporting the brand's growth across the Middle East and Europe. She also founded **Semsom,** a modern Lebanese restaurant concept, along with other ventures like Green Falafel and Home in a Bite.

Christine advises companies on growth, franchising, and strategy in markets including Lebanon, the UAE, Saudi Arabia, and others. **She serves on the YPO Global Retail Network Board** supporting 4000+ retail CEOs across the world.

A lifelong advocate for women, Christine has mentored thousands of female entrepreneurs and leaders through her programs: **The Empowering Tribe, The Spark Program, Her Book Club, and Corporate Workshops,** with a mission to impact **100,000 women** through strategy, mindset, and leadership.

She holds degrees from **AUB, McGill, ESA, Harvard Business School**, with additional executive studies at **Stanford** and **London Business School.** Her work has earned her titles like **Middle East Businesswoman of the Year (2011)** and a spot on **Forbes Middle East** and **Arabian Business's** lists of the **100 Most Powerful Arab Women** for seven years in a row.

Beyond business, Christine is an adventurer; the **first Middle Eastern person to reach the North Pole,** proudly planting the Lebanese flag in a skydiving expedition, with **389 jumps so far,** visited **81 countries** (targeting 100 soon!), and a past life as a private pilot and rally driver. But above all, she's proudest of being a **mother to two amazing daughters.**

# UNDERSTANDING THE
# LANDSCAPE

# THE CAREER EQUATION IS DIFFERENT FOR WOMEN

Let's talk about the obvious, the thing most of us sense as we grow in our professional lives, even if no one says it out loud:

## Men and women don't experience careers the same way.

On paper, the journey might start the same. We graduate. We land a job. We work hard. We climb the ladder. But not long after that, the paths begin to diverge; not because of a lack of ambition or ability, but because of how deeply personal life choices impact our professional ones.

For most men, the career path is a straight line. It's expected, encouraged, uninterrupted. They go from assistant manager to manager, to director, to maybe launching their own business. And all along the way, everyone around them; family, friends, society supports that progression as the priority.

For women? The line isn't straight. It zigzags. It pauses. It curves. And not because we're any less committed or capable, but because our lives are more intertwined with major personal milestones that deeply affect how and when we work.

Let's break it down.

After graduating, many women start their careers just like men. But then, choices come into play. **Marriage** is often the first fork in the road. Some women continue working full-time. Others decide to pause, shift to part-time, or even step away from the workforce; sometimes by choice, sometimes by expectation.

Then comes **pregnancy;** another major turning point. Some women continue working without a hitch. Others need rest, more flexibility, or choose to focus on their health and baby. There's no one right way, but again, it's a moment where decisions about career become deeply personal.

Once children are born, the challenges intensify. **Raising young kids** is a beautiful, exhausting, all-consuming job. And while some women power through with full-time roles, others scale back. Not because they don't care about their careers, but because they're trying to balance two full-time roles at once. It's not about choosing family over work; it's often about finding a way to make both fit, without burning out.

Then comes the second child. Maybe a third. For some, more. Each phase brings new dynamics, more demands, and often, more career pauses or adjustments. I've had conversations with hundreds of women. Some continue working full-time. Others pivot into entrepreneurship during this phase, seeking more control over their time. Many choose freelancing. And some step away entirely for a season.
But it doesn't stop there.

By our late 30s and into our 40s and 50s, we enter **perimenopause;** something rarely talked about in the workplace, yet very real. It can start as early as 35 and last into our 50s or even 60s. It brings hormonal shifts, physical changes, mood swings, brain fog, and yes, the occasional hot flash in the middle of a meeting or workshop (ask me how I know).

Again, these aren't weaknesses. They're just **realities.** And they affect how we show up at work, how we plan, and how we make decisions.

So, what's the point of all this?

The point is: **Awareness is power.**

When you understand that your career won't follow a straight line; and that this isn't a problem to be "fixed," but a truth to be navigated; you can make decisions without guilt. Without shame. Without feeling like a failure or a victim.

That's what I've seen over and over again in my work with thousands of women. So many of us carry guilt. Guilt for stepping back. Guilt for wanting more. Guilt for not "doing it all." And on the other side? Victimhood. Feeling like we're trapped by our biology, our roles, or our responsibilities.
But here's the truth: **we are not victims, and we don't need to feel guilty.**
We just need to become conscious decision-makers.

Yes, there are more layers. Yes, the path is messier. But the beauty of being a woman today is that there are **many ways to shape a meaningful, successful life.** The challenge is not in choosing the "perfect" path; it's in giving ourselves permission to choose our path.

In the next chapters, we're going to dig into the **different options** available to you. We'll talk about what each one looks like, what the trade-offs are, and how to set up your life, practically and mentally, to live with joy, intention, and freedom.

The straight line? That's one version of success. But it's not the only one. And for most women, it's not even the most fulfilling one.

Your path might bend, pause, stretch, or loop. That's not a problem.

That's just a different kind of power.

---

# A MISSION WORTH PURSUING

If you're a woman reading this, chances are you've felt guilt. Not once, not twice, but probably every single day.

I know I did.

Guilty for not spending enough time with my kids when I was at work.

Guilty for not being fully present at work because I was thinking about my kids.

Guilty for not seeing my parents enough, not calling a friend back, not taking care of myself properly.

Guilty for resting. Guilty for working. Guilty for... everything.

It was like I was carrying this invisible backpack filled with little guilt pebbles, and every day I just kept adding to it.

### The Wake-Up Moment:
# LIVING THE PRESENT FULLY

The turning point came when I read about the importance of living fully in the moment. That single idea, **presence over perfection,** changed everything for me.

So I made a new decision.

When I'm at work, I'm fully at work. My family knows that unless it's truly urgent, I'm focused and present.
When I'm home, my phone goes on silent and face-down. I'm fully there, for my kids, my partner, my family.

When I'm with friends, it's the same. Eye contact, laughter, presence. In those moments, I'm not an entrepreneur or a mom, I'm just their friend.

And guess what?

That alone did wonders to remove the guilt.

Because guilt thrives in the gap between where we are and where we think we "should" be.

Presence kills the guilt.

Living each moment fully is the antidote.

# WHAT THERAPY TAUGHT ME ABOUT GUILT

Years later, during a therapy session, my therapist said something that struck me like lightning:

"Guilt helps no one. It doesn't help your kids. It doesn't help your career. It doesn't help your soul. It only weighs you down."

It made me pause. And reflect. Because we often think that guilt is noble, that it means we care.

But **guilt is not love.**

**Guilt is not responsibility.**

**Guilt is not purpose.**

It's a drain. A distraction. A way to sabotage our presence and joy.

And once you see it that way; as *useless*; you start letting it go.

**The Bhutan Story:**
# WHEN GUILT DOESN'T EXIST

Let me share one of the most powerful experiences I've had around this topic.

I was in Bhutan, hiking 12 kilometers up a mountain to a sacred monastery called the Tiger's Nest. After hours of walking, we finally arrived at the top and had a rare opportunity to speak to a wise monk.

A few of us got to ask him questions. I asked how I could feel okay enjoying myself on this trip when my parents were in Lebanon, and things weren't great back home. Another woman shared that she felt guilty for being here while her kids were back home.
We expected wisdom. But what we got was wonder; because the monk simply didn't understand the concept of guilt!

Not because he didn't speak English.

He was fluent.

But because guilt as a concept was foreign to him.
We tried for 10 minutes to explain it. With Google Translate, with metaphors, with examples. And when he finally grasped what we meant, he looked at us and said:

"But why would you do that to yourself? You are here now. This is what matters."

It was such a wake-up call. Guilt is not universal. Guilt is *learned*. It's cultural. And maybe it's time to *unlearn* it.

# A MISSION TO KILL THE GUILT

If this book can help you do one thing, I hope it's this:
Let go of the guilt.

Replace it with presence. Replace it with clear decisions. Replace it with love.

Love for yourself. Love for your choices. Love for the life you're creating, imperfect as it may be.

Here's what I've learned:

- You're allowed to be focused on work without guilt.
- You're allowed to rest without guilt.
- You're allowed to say no without guilt.
- You're allowed to buy yourself the bag you want without guilt.
- You're allowed to change your mind without guilt.
- You're allowed to be where you are and nowhere else.

This isn't easy. It takes practice.

But it's possible. And it's worth it.

So consider this your personal invitation:

Join me in being on a mission to kill the guilt.

To say YES to presence, purpose, and peace.

You deserve that. And so do the people who love you.

# LEARNING FROM OTHERS, BUT CHOSSING FOR YOURSELF

In the next chapters, we're going to explore real examples of different life and career trahectories that women have taken. Not as blueprints to copy, but as mirrors and windows.

# CHRIS' STORY; CHOOSING AMBITION WITHOUT GUILT

Let me introduce you to Chris. She may sound familiar; and that's no coincidence. Her story is my story, and the first of several paths we'll explore in this book.

Chris was focused. From a young age, she made education her top priority. She pursued her studies with intention and excellence, and even after launching her first business at 22, her commitment to learning never stopped.

When she got married, she was already building her career. She loved what she was creating; the energy of it, the freedom, the growth. And importantly, her decision to keep growing her business while married wasn't just hers alone; it was a shared agreement with her husband. They had the conversation early: What kind of life do we want to build? What role will each of us play? What does support look like?

# THIS IS A KEY POINT FOR ANYONE PLANNING TO BUILD A LIFE WITH A PARTNER.

*Talk about your vision for work, family, and balance early on. Alignment at the foundation prevents conflict later.*

Chris chose to keep building, keep growing, keep traveling. She enjoyed the pace of her life; business meetings, weekend trips, long workouts. And when the thought of having children came up, she hesitated. Not because she didn't want them, but because she loved her life as it was, and she knew having kids would change things.

Eventually, she decided it was time and was blessed to become pregnant. She was thrilled. Out of everything she has done, this turned out to be the best blessing in her life. But she didn't stop. She traveled, worked, led teams. Until one day, her body said: Enough. She was grounded, placed on bed rest for the final two months of her pregnancy (and four months for the second one).

At first, she felt herself slipping into a downward spiral, but she quickly paused, regrouped, and adapted.

With fewer distractions and interruptions than a normal workday, Chris found herself unusually productive. She got creative. She restructured. She stayed in motion; just differently.

Three weeks after her daughter was born, Chris was back at work. But this wasn't a case of "doing it all" alone. She had a setup. A system. And that made all the difference.

Here's what that looked like:

- Her mother stepped in to help every afternoon, offering not just emotional support but hands-on care. Until now, the kids have an amazing relation with her.
- She had a nanny at home, and didn't carry the burden of housework; she outsourced cooking, cleaning, laundry.
- She was strategic with her time: Every Sunday, she planned the week's meals, ordered groceries, and organized her schedule so she could focus on work and family without being buried in logistics.
- A driver helped get the kids to activities safely and efficiently.

## TODAY'S LESSON

**You can't do both full-speed career and full-time parenting alone. You need support; and a system.**

But what really helped her stay grounded wasn't just the help. It was clarity.

Chris saw a child therapist regularly; not because anything was wrong, but because she wanted to understand what her children actually needed at each stage. And she learned something that changed everything:

"Young children don't need you all the time. But when you're with them, they need you fully."

That became her guiding principle.

Before walking into the house, she'd take a few quiet minutes in the car; to reset, breathe, disconnect from work. Once inside, the phone was off. Her attention was 100% on her child. Even if it was just one hour, it was present, intentional, uninterrupted time.

As her daughters grew, Chris continued adjusting. She delegated more, refocused her time, and re-evaluated what mattered most at each stage of life and business.

And here's what made all of it possible; and joyful. She dropped the guilt and had clarity of what she wanted.

## WHAT CHRIS'S STORY TEACHES US

This path isn't for everyone. Full-time work, full-time parenting, and full-speed ambition; all at once; is a big choice. But for those who want it, it's possible. Not without help. Not without planning. But absolutely possible.

And the most important part? You get to choose. Not because someone told you what a "good mom" or "good woman" looks like. But because you know what lights you up; and you've built your life to support it.

In the next chapters, we'll meet other women who made very different choices. Slower pace. Full-time parenting. Creative pivots. Late bloomers. Because there isn't one right way.

There's only the way that feels right for you.

# ASKING FOR HELP IS A STRENGTH

One of the most powerful lessons I've learned, both as a mother and as an entrepreneur, is that asking for help is not a sign of weakness. In fact, it's a quiet act of strength, self-awareness, and humility.

I couldn't have built my career, grown my businesses, or stayed true to my mission without the incredible support system around me. My mom was by my side every single afternoon for years with my daughters, while I poured myself into building something I believed in. I'll be forever grateful. But I also know that not everyone has that kind of help built-in.

Sometimes your support system won't be your mom. It might be a sibling, a cousin, a neighbor, a friend, or even someone from a community you choose to join. But the truth remains: we're not meant to do life alone, especially not the version of life where we dare to dream big, take risks, and juggle multiple roles with passion and purpose.

This applies in business too. As an entrepreneur, you will face moments of doubt, struggle, and even burnout. Having people around you who understand what you're going through can be the difference between giving up and growing through it.

If you don't already have a built-in support network, it's never too late to build one. That's why communities like The Empowering Tribe exist, to offer a safe space where women leaders can uplift each other. We celebrate wins together, and we hold each other through the hard days. We offer perspective, encouragement, wisdom, and most importantly, presence.

Real friends, real allies, are not just the ones who show up for the celebrations. They're the ones who show up when your world feels like it's falling apart. The ones who help you breathe, see clearly, and find the next step forward.

And don't forget, support is a two-way street. Be there for others. Be the person who listens without judgment. Who offers time, perspective, or simply a shoulder. Because the day you need it most, your community will rise for you too.

So don't hesitate to ask for help. It doesn't make you less capable. It makes you human. And it makes your journey lighter, richer, and more connected.

---

# NADIA'S STORY; REDEFINING GROWTH ON HER OWN TERMS

# **MEET** NADIA.

Nadia is sharp, ambitious, and deeply committed to her career. She works full-time in a corporate role, and she's excellent at what she does. She also has a family, young children, and a strong desire to be present in both parts of her life; professional and personal.

But unlike Chris, Nadia's struggle isn't about whether she can do both. It's about the cost of trying to keep up with a career trajectory that wasn't built with women's realities in mind.

She found herself in a workplace where the career path was linear and uninterrupted; a system designed around the traditional male journey. Graduate, work full-time, take on stretch projects, climb the ladder, never pause, never slow down.

And Nadia tried to match that pace.

She pushed through meetings while pumping milk in the bathroom. She answered emails from hospital waiting rooms. She took calls during school pickups. On the outside, she looked like she was keeping up. But on the inside, she often felt like she was drowning; and what made it worse was the quiet sense that she was failing at both.

And that's when the guilt crept in. And not just guilt; **resentment.** She began to feel like a victim. Like no matter how hard she tried, the system was stacked against her. That others, mostly men, didn't have to make these trade-offs, or prove themselves again and again after each maternity leave, sick day, or school emergency.

But then something shifted.

Nadia started seeing her situation not just as a struggle; but as a set of **choices.**

"It's not about what the system expects. It's about what I want; and what I'm willing to give for it."

She realized she had a few different paths:

# PATH 1
## Keep Up with the "Standard" Pace

If she wanted to grow quickly and stay in line for every promotion, she could do it. But she'd need a structure. Like Chris, she'd need real support at home and at work. And she'd have to make a conscious decision to stay partially engaged even during maternity leave; maybe two to three hours a day to stay in the loop with her team and clients. It's not ideal, but it's one version of the trade-off.

# PATH 2
## Take the Break

Alternatively, Nadia could use her maternity leave as a true pause. No emails. No updates. Full presence with her baby. But that meant accepting that when she came back, the company may have moved on. She might not be in line for the next promotion right away. She might need time to catch up. And that's okay; if it's a choice she owns.

Because **this is what changed for Nadia:** she stopped feeling like a victim. She stopped believing that everything was happening to her. She started owning the fact that she was choosing; not being forced.

> "If I want the promotion, I'll need to stay engaged. If I want the pause, I'll take it; and I'll re-enter at my pace. Either way, it's mine."

This shift in mindset was everything.

---

## LET'S TALK ABOUT THE VICTIM MINDSET

Feeling like a victim is common; and it's understandable. Especially in systems that weren't built for the modern working mother. But it's also dangerous.

Because the moment you feel like a victim, you give away your power.

You start believing that you don't have control; and that's the quickest way to feel stuck, bitter, or burned out.

Let's be clear: life is not always fair. The world isn't always supportive. But you are still the driver of your journey.

- If you want the promotion; you'll need to show up for it, even if it means working part-time during leave.
- If you want a season of peace; you can take it, without guilt, and without thinking you've lost your edge.
- If you want to grow slower; that's growth, too.

There's no prize for who climbs the ladder fastest. Your path, your pace, your values.

The only thing that really matters is this: Did you choose it?

Because when you choose; even the hard things, you feel empowered. You feel in control. And that's the difference between burning out and growing through the challenge.

One of the comments I hear often is:

"But I still have to do the work; I have bills to pay. I'm not exactly doing my dream job, but I don't really have a choice right now."

And to that, I say: you're absolutely right, we can't always be living our ideal life 100% of the time. **There are seasons when we do what we must in order to eventually do what we love.** That doesn't make you a victim; it makes you committed.

If you're in a job that isn't your passion, but you're using it to build the financial stability for you and your family or seed money you need to start your business, pivot careers, or fund a dream; that's not settling. That's planning. That's strategy. That's strength.

The difference lies in the story you tell yourself. If you say, "I hate my job, I feel stuck, I'm wasting my life," that's victim energy. But if you reframe it as, "This job is my stepping stone. It's temporary. I'm saving. I'm building. I have a plan," that's powerful. That's ownership.

You don't need to love every task or every season of your life. But when your actions are aligned with a larger purpose, even if the current chapter isn't perfect, you're still on the path. You're still saying yes to the life you're building.

# WHAT NADIA'S STORY TEACHES US

Nadia didn't quit her job. She didn't burn out. She didn't explode in frustration. Instead, she paused. She reflected. And she started choosing from a place of clarity; not pressure.

And that clarity allowed her to redefine what success meant for her: maybe not getting every promotion right away, but growing sustainably while staying present with her kids. It meant releasing the guilt and comparison, and embracing the idea that she could build a career at her pace; not someone else's.

If you saw yourself in Nadia's story, know this: you're not alone. And more importantly, you're not stuck. You have options. You have power. And you have the right to decide what balance, growth, and success look like in your own life.

In the next chapter, we'll meet someone who made a very different choice; someone who chose to step away completely for a while. Another valid path. Another way to say yes to a happy, meaningful life.

# NOOR'S STORY;
# A SEASON FOR EVERYTHING

# MEET NOOR.

She was brilliant. Graduated with honors. Landed an incredible job at a company where she felt challenged, seen, and impactful. She was proud of her work; the projects she led, the people she mentored, the impact she made.

Then life took a turn; a beautiful one. She met someone. They fell in love. Got married. And when she became pregnant with her first child, Noor made a decision that changed everything:

> **She chose to become a full-time, stay-at-home mom.**

It wasn't a fallback plan. It wasn't out of pressure. It was a choice; one made in full alignment with her husband, and one she felt deeply at peace with.

And for the first few years, Noor was truly happy. She embraced it fully.

- She was there for every milestone: the first steps, the first words, the endless questions.
- She went to every school activity, every birthday party, every bake sale.
- She built deep friendships with other stay-at-home moms.
- Her days were full of playgrounds, storybooks, scraped knees, and sticky fingers; and she loved it.

This is what I wanted; to be fully present for these magical,

**fleeting years.**

And then… time passed.

One child became two. Then three. Life was rich, warm, loud. And then one day, the youngest started school.

And for the first time in years, the house was quiet.
That's when it hit her: **a deep, unfamiliar void.**

The calendar was suddenly empty. The routines that had once felt so full were now over. She began to ask herself:

- What do I do now?
- Did I waste the past six or seven years?
- Have I fallen too far behind to start again?

And most painfully:

**Who am I now, beyond "Mom"?**

# A TURNING POINT: FROM VOID TO VISION

For a little while, Noor felt lost. She slipped into that common trap: looking back at her decision, one she once felt so good about, and questioning it. She started comparing herself to former colleagues who had kept climbing while she was knee-deep in diapers and snack boxes.

She started to feel like a failure.

Until one day, she attended a mindset workshop. It wasn't earth-shattering; no grand epiphany. But something simple clicked:

> "This is my life. These were my choices. And I was proud of them then; I can still be proud of them now."

She stopped asking what she missed, and started asking:

What's next?

As she stepped back and re-evaluated, Noor saw she had options; and that's when things started to feel exciting again.

## OPTION 1
# RE-ENTER THE WORKFORCE WITH NEW SKILLS

Yes, she'd been out of the corporate world for a while. Yes, that was a challenge. But instead of trying to "catch up" in the same lane, Noor pivoted. She asked herself:

*What do I enjoy? What am I naturally good at?*

The answer for her: **negotiation**.

So she dove in, took courses, attended workshops, even earned a diploma in negotiation. Slowly, she built her confidence and network. Eventually, she re-entered the workforce not just as a returning mom; but as a subject matter expert in her field.

## OPTION 2
# BUILD SOMETHING NEW

Another path Noor could have taken, and one many women do, **is starting something from scratch.** Often, the best ideas come from our own pain points. Noor had lived the day-to-day challenges of motherhood, and through that, discovered problems worth solving.

She could've launched a business that served parents like her, a platform, a product, a service, and grown it from idea to **multi-million-dollar brand.**

Because when your business solves your problem, you're naturally your best customer, marketer, and founder.

## OPTION 3
# FOLLOW HER PASSION

And a third path: passion-driven purpose. For some women, this next season isn't about climbing or building; it's about expression. Noor could have discovered a passion for **well-being, education, travel, or social impact;** and channeled that into something deeply fulfilling, such as:

- Becoming a certified life coach
- Leading yoga retreats or wellness workshops
- Volunteering or starting a non-profit
- Organizing meaningful group trips for women
- Writing, teaching, mentoring

The possibilities were endless, not because she "needed" to make up for lost time, but because she was stepping into a new season with intention.

# WHAT NOOR'S STORY TEACHES US

There's a season for everything.

Noor's choice to pause her career wasn't a step back. It was a conscious decision to be fully present for a chapter that mattered to her. And later, when that chapter evolved, she made another decision: to rediscover herself.

She didn't let the six or seven years define what was no longer possible. Instead, she used that time as a foundation for what came next.

You don't have to choose once. You can choose again.

**And again.
And again.**

If you see yourself in Noor, know this:

- It's okay to pause.
- It's okay to change.
- It's okay to want more, or something entirely different.

Motherhood doesn't erase your identity. It adds depth to it.

And your second act can be just as powerful, or even more, than your first.

# THE POWER OF RECEIVING

There's something many of us were never really taught: how to receive.

Not just gifts or compliments, but support, love, help, care. Somewhere along the way, we learned that receiving was a weakness. That to be strong meant to do it all ourselves. That "I've got this" was a badge of honor.

I've lived this. And I've seen it over and over again in the women around me, this **I can do it myself** syndrome.

It shows up in the smallest ways. When someone tries to open a door for you and you say, "No, no, I got it." When someone offers to help carry your luggage and you refuse. When your partner wants to buy you a gift and your first instinct is to say, "It's not the right time. We have school fees to pay." We brush it off, we minimize, we deflect.

But what if I told you that **receiving is not weakness, it's a skill?** One that we all need to practice more.

I remember a workshop I attended where the facilitator said something that hit me deeply: "When you constantly say no to receiving, you're not just rejecting support, you're denying others the joy of giving." That was a wake-up call. I had been so focused on giving, giving my time, my energy, my love, that I hadn't realized how uncomfortable I was with receiving.

So I started small. I said thank you when someone held the door. I smiled and accepted help with my bags on a flight. I let my daughters pamper me on Mother's Day. And slowly, something shifted. I felt lighter. More connected. More balanced.

Because here's the truth: **Receiving is part of the feminine energy that balances our masculine drive.** And as women who are often in leadership roles, managing families, building businesses, we carry a lot of masculine energy, structure, action, doing. That's amazing. It's powerful.

But we also need the softness. **The surrender.** The joy of being taken care of.

And this brings me to something else I struggled with, and that many strong women will relate to: **the challenge of being strong at work and soft at home.**

When you're so used to being the one who leads, decides, pushes forward, it can be hard to switch off that energy in your personal life. To let myself be cared for. To lean back. I was always in "go" mode, always planning, doing, fixing. Being a "princess"? That felt foreign.

But I've learned that **being pampered, being cherished, doesn't take away from your strength. It adds to it.**

Being able to soften, to rest, to receive, that is strength, too.

It doesn't make you any less ambitious, or smart, or powerful. It just means you're embracing your full self. You can lead meetings and still enjoy being taken out to dinner. You can manage a team and still love when someone surprises you with flowers.

You can be the queen and the princess. The nurturer and the one who is nurtured.

So let me ask you: **when was the last time you really allowed yourself to receive?**

If this is something you struggle with, you are not alone.

Try this: start small. Say thank you. Smile. Let people give. Let your partner take care of you. Let your friends support you. Say yes to joy, to ease, to softness. You deserve it.

And remember, receiving doesn't mean you're not strong. **It means you're strong enough to know you don't have to do it all alone.**

---

# RANA'S STORY; CHOOSING PURPOSE OVER CONVENTION

# LET'S MEET RANA.

Like the other women you've read about, she started off strong. Great education. Sharp mind. Driven by excellence. She entered the workforce and, step by step, climbed the corporate ladder. Promotions, responsibilities, accolades; she earned them all.

But something was off.

On the outside, everything looked great. On the inside, she was running on fumes.

Eventually, Rana hit a wall. Burnout. Deep, disorienting, soul-draining burnout. The kind that doesn't just make you tired, it makes you question everything.

She had spent years chasing a version of success that, somewhere along the way, stopped feeling like hers.

So she did something brave:

She stopped. And pivoted.

Rana left the corporate world. She took time to breathe. To rest. To reflect. And eventually, she decided to start her own business; something more aligned with her energy and values. It wasn't easy, but it felt real. She was building something on her terms.
Along the way, Rana experienced another set of pressures: relationships that didn't work out, expectations around marriage and motherhood, conversations that made her feel like she was somehow "late" or "missing out."

But here's the thing: Rana wasn't missing anything.

She just didn't want the same things others did. And after enough time trying to make conventional paths work, she got clear on her truth:

**"I don't want to get married. I don't want to have kids. I want to dedicate my life to something bigger than myself."**

And she did.

# A LIFE OF IMPACT

Rana committed her life to a cause that broke her heart and fired up her spirit: child hunger.

She had seen firsthand how many children go to bed without food, and how easily it could be changed with the right systems, support, and action.

So she threw herself into that mission.

- She worked with grassroots organizations and international NGOs.
- She launched awareness campaigns and fundraising initiatives.
- She helped design school lunch programs in underserved communities.
- She built partnerships that led to real, measurable impact.

Rana wasn't raising children of her own; she was helping thousands of children survive, thrive, and believe in a better future.

Her calendar wasn't filled with playdates. It was filled with strategy calls, food distribution schedules, travel to remote regions, and speaking events.

And she loved it.

This was her happy, meaningful life. No guilt. No apologies. No regrets.

# WHAT RANA'S STORY TEACHES US

We live in a world that often tells women there's one version of happiness:

- Find a partner.
- Raise a family.
- Build a "balanced" life.

But the truth is, there are many versions of happiness; and not all of them include marriage, children, or the traditional milestones. Rana didn't reject those things out of bitterness. She chose a different path because she knew what mattered to her most, and she gave herself permission to follow it fully.

And that's the key: permission.

Permission to not explain yourself.

Permission to prioritize purpose.

Permission to be a woman whose life is filled with meaning, even if it looks nothing like anyone else's.

# A NOTE TO THE READER

If you saw yourself in Rana's story, even just a little, let this be your reminder:

- You are not behind.
- You are not broken.
- You are not missing anything.

You are designing a life that reflects you. And the world needs women like Rana; women who break the mold, challenge the norms, and devote themselves to work that leaves a mark.

Your version of a meaningful life is valid, important, and enough.

# BREAKING FREE FROM LIMITING BELIEFS

A limiting belief is a state of mind, conviction, or internalized narrative that you believe to be true, but that, in reality, holds you back. It can influence how you see yourself, what you think you're capable of, and what kind of life you believe you deserve. These beliefs act like invisible barriers that block growth, success, and happiness.

What's important to understand is: we all have limiting beliefs. Every single one of us. And that's okay. What matters is our awareness. Because once you notice the belief, you can begin to challenge it.

Some common limiting beliefs sound like:

- "I'm too old for this."
- "I'm too young to be taken seriously."
- "I have too many degrees, I am overqualified."
- "I don't have enough degrees."
- "I've missed my chance."
- "I don't have what it takes."
- "People like me don't do things like that."
- "If I fail, I'll prove everyone right."

Here's the twist: your brain is wired to prove you right. If you tell yourself, I'm not good enough, your brain will actively search for evidence to support that thought.

But the exact same mechanism works in your favor when you switch the narrative: I am capable. I'm just getting started. I've got this. Your brain will then go looking for evidence to support that truth, too.

# THE WORLD RECORD ANALOGY

A great example is the way world records are broken. For years, people believed it was impossible to run a 100m in under 10 seconds. Then someone did it. Within months, others broke the same record. What changed? Not the human body. The belief. Once people saw it was possible, they allowed themselves to believe they could do it too.

# WHERE DO LIMITING BELIEFS COME FROM?

Limiting beliefs are often formed in childhood or early adulthood:

- Maybe a teacher once told you that you weren't smart enough.
- Maybe you grew up hearing that "money doesn't grow on trees," or that "rich people are greedy," and now you subconsciously reject financial success.
- Maybe one failed project or rejection led you to conclude, I'm not cut out for this.

You didn't choose these beliefs; but you can choose whether to keep them.

# QUICK EXERCISE: IDENTIFY YOUR TOP 3 LIMITING BELIEFS

Take a few minutes. Write down:

1.  What do I believe is holding me back right now?
2.  What do I tell myself I can't do; and why?
3.  What messages or stories have I internalized from others (parents, school, society)?

Then ask:

·   Is this 100% true?
·   Would I say this to someone I love?
·   What's a more empowering belief I can choose instead?

Once you shine a light on a limiting belief, it begins to lose its power. That belief is not you. It's just a sentence in your mind, and you have the ability to change the script.

Let this be your reminder: you are more powerful than the stories you've been told. It's time to write your own.

# CHAPTER 6

# LEYLA'S STORY; CHOOSING ENERGY AND PURPOSE OVER CONVENTIONAL PATH

# MEET LEYLA.

Leyla's story is one of clarity, calm, confidence, and deep inner work. From a young age, Leyla had a strong sense of who she wanted to become. She was naturally drawn to personal growth, diving into books, workshops, and coaching programs that helped her build powerful inner foundations: mindset, emotional regulation, energy management, and spiritual connection. She wasn't good at school and dropped out of university.

Unlike many who hustle from morning to night, Leyla took a very intentional approach to her life. She knew from experience that doing more didn't always mean achieving more, and that her energy was her most precious currency. She chose to build a business that aligned with her purpose and ran it with elegance and efficiency. Her golden rule? Focus only on what matters most, and delegate the rest.

Leyla became known as the "queen of delegation." She surrounded herself with the right team, the right support at home, and the right systems so that her working hours rarely exceeded four focused hours a day. In those hours, she made bold decisions, drove strategy, and empowered others to execute. And the rest of the time, she was focused on her kids, her husband, her friends without forgetting herself.

But Leyla didn't just build a business, she built a life. Every morning, she started her day with intention. Whether it was a long walk, a workout, meditation, journaling, or spiritual connection, her daily rituals helped her stay grounded and connected to her higher self. She carved out at least two hours a day for self-care and protected those boundaries fiercely.

When life called for change, Leyla didn't resist. She had trained herself to see pivots not as failures but as invitations, to grow, to explore, to evolve. Whether it was shifting business direction, letting go of a partnership, or moving into a new phase of life, she moved with faith. Deep down, she trusted that the universe had her back. God had her back. And that inner certainty gave her the freedom to say yes to new opportunities and no to anything that drained her.

Leyla never aimed to "do it all." She simply designed a life that was fully aligned with her values, a life that gave her time for family, space for stillness, and room to thrive.

# WHAT WE LEARN FROM LEYLA

Leyla's path teaches us that clarity is power, and that when we trust ourselves, we can build extraordinary lives, on our own terms.

But perhaps the biggest lesson lies in how she felt about herself.

So many women I've worked with struggle with the same two feelings: "I'm not good enough" and "I'm not worth it." These inner voices are often louder than any external pressure. And unless we learn to quiet them, they shape our decisions, our confidence, and our sense of what's possible.

Leyla's story reminds us that self-worth is not something we earn, it's something we remember.

When we accept ourselves exactly as we are, with all the imperfections, all the beauty, all the mess, and when we root ourselves in the truth that we are deeply connected to God, to the universe, to something greater... we tap into limitless power. We begin to move not from fear or proving, but from peace and purpose.

So whatever your journey looks like, start here:

You are enough. You are worthy. You are powerful beyond measure. And when you believe that, you'll make choices that reflect it, and create a life that feels like yours

# I AM ENOUGH: REWRITING THE INNER NARRATIVE

Of all the emotions that quietly weigh on women's shoulders: guilt, overwhelm, feeling like a victim… there's one that runs deeper, often hiding under the surface:

The feeling of not being enough.

It can show up subtly or fiercely.

"I'm not a good enough mom."
"I'm not smart enough to lead this project."
"I'm not experienced enough to launch this business."
"I'm not attractive enough. Not patient enough. Not brave enough…"

This belief shows up everywhere, in our relationships, our careers, our parenting, even in the way we take care of ourselves.

And when you believe you're not enough, something dangerous starts to happen:

You begin to settle.

You stay in relationships that don't nourish your soul.

You stay in jobs that drain you because you don't believe something better is possible.

You stop dreaming. You stop expanding. You begin to shrink.

# THE TRUTH: YOU WERE ALWAYS ENOUGH

Here's what I want you to hear, truly and deeply:
You were born enough.

You were created whole. Everything you need is already inside you.

But somewhere along the way, through culture, upbringing, comparison, trauma, media, little voices crept in. And those voices weren't even yours. But over time, you started believing them.

What if you could stop believing them?
What if you could talk back?

## TALKING TO YOUR THOUGHTS

One of the most powerful mindset tools I've learned, and that I teach in my workshops, is this:

Your thoughts are not facts.

Let me say that again: **Your thoughts are not facts.**

They are just stories your brain repeats over and over again, and you have the power to challenge them. To change them.

The voice that says, "You're not good enough," is trying to protect you. It's trying to keep you safe, hidden, small, so you don't risk embarrassment or failure.

But you can thank that voice. You can talk back.

"Thank you for trying to protect me. But I've got this. I'm going to try anyway. I'm going to show up, imperfect, but powerful."

# HOW THE BRAIN WORKS:

Here's something that truly changed my life:

Your brain is wired to prove you right.

If you tell yourself, "I'm a loser"; your brain will filter reality to show you why that's true.

If you tell yourself, "I'm enough, I'm powerful, I attract beautiful opportunities"; your brain will filter for that too.

This is called the Reticular Activating System, it's the brain's filter. It decides what information to let in and what to delete. That's why if you say you want to buy a red car, suddenly you see red cars everywhere.

The red cars were always there, your brain just hadn't been told to notice them.

That's the power of affirmations. It's not fiction. It's neuroscience.

Train your brain to work for you, not against you.

# TRY THESE AFFIRMATIONS

Repeat them. Write them. Say them aloud every morning. Whisper them before bed. Let them rewire your mind.

- I am enough.
- I am safe.
- I am deeply loved.
- I am whole, just as I am.
- I attract abundance and joy.
- Opportunities flow to me effortlessly.
- I am worthy of rest, success, love, wealth, and peace.

And when the doubt still comes, because it will, talk to it like a loving friend.

"I hear you. But I choose a different story today."

# BECAUSE ONCE YOU BELIEVE YOU'RE ENOUGH...

...you stop settling.

You stop apologizing for taking up space.

You stop hiding and start living, boldly, joyfully, unapologetically.

You lead. You create. You inspire. You attract.

You begin to show others that they are enough too, simply by being yourself.

So, if there's one thing I want you to walk away with from this book, it's this:

You are already enough.

Let your story start there.

# CONCLUSION TO PART I
## YOUR LIFE, YOUR YES

We could keep going.

We could tell you the stories of dozens more women: different backgrounds, different choices, different definitions of success. Because the truth is, there's no one-size-fits-all. No single formula. No "best" trajectory.

And I would love you to share your story! Just email your story to story@catalystofgrowth.com and we will be sharing more stories along the way.

To show that:

Some women build businesses.

Some raise children full-time.

Some climb the corporate ladder.

Some start over at 45.

Some travel the world.

Some stay rooted in one place.

Some choose partnership.

Some do all of the above; at different points in life.
There's no right or wrong.

No timeline.

No universal checklist.

This is **the power to say yes;** the power of being a woman in today's world, where you can define your life path, your values, your rhythm. You don't have to follow someone else's script. You can write your own.

That's why I wanted to show you these stories; Chris, Nadia, Noor, Rana and Leyla. Each one different. Each one valid. And each one making choices that felt aligned with their season, their values, their truth.

And now, it's your turn.

You are not too early. Not too late. Not too old. Not too young. Not under qualified or overqualified.

You are exactly where you need to be, with the power to decide what comes next.

Now that you have clarity, you're ready for the next step:

Designing your happy, meaningful life.
Not based on what the world expects.
Not based on guilt or pressure.
But based on you.

Let's begin.

# PART 2

# DESIGNING THE LIFE YOU WANT

# CHAPTER 7

# DESIGNING YOUR LIFE; THE POWER OF PROTOTYPING YOUR FUTURE

We often talk about life as something that happens to us, circumstances, luck, obligations, timing. But what if you approached your life the way a designer approaches a product? With intention. With creativity. With the power to prototype, test, and adapt?

This is the mindset behind one of the most powerful frameworks I've ever encountered: Designing Your Life, a methodology created at Stanford University's Design Thinking School. I had the privilege of attending a workshop there, and it completely transformed how I think about life planning.

Here's what makes it so brilliant, it doesn't ask you to choose one perfect path. Instead, it invites you to explore multiple versions of your future, reflect on what matters most, and start designing a life that aligns with your values, energy, and vision of fulfillment.

Whether you're 25 or 55, whether you're in a career sprint or on a pause, this framework helps you pause and ask the question we so rarely stop to consider:

What do I actually want my life to look like?

Let's dive into the three-life exercise.

# STEP 1
## Understand the Concept of Life Design

Designers build solutions around people, not assumptions. They don't try to solve everything at once. They prototype. They play. They test. They design.

That's exactly how we can approach our own lives.

Instead of trying to find the "one right answer," we can explore a few different directions, see what energizes us, and then consciously design a life that includes the best parts of all of them.

And just like a product, your life design evolves. You're not locked into one version forever. You can iterate. Adapt. Reimagine. But first, you need to explore what's actually possible.

# STEP 2
## Create Three Versions of Your Life

Grab a notebook, a journal, or a piece of paper. Give yourself some quiet time to think, feel, and imagine. You're going to write three different five-year life plans, not from a place of fear or pressure, but from a place of curiosity.

Let yourself dream.

# LIFE #1
## The Perfect Current Path

Imagine that everything in your current life goes beautifully. No major disruptions. No dramatic changes. You keep doing what you're doing, but it works. Your work grows. Your relationships deepen. Your lifestyle improves. It's the best-case version of the life you're already living.

Ask yourself:

- What kind of work am I doing?
- Where am I living?
- Who am I spending time with every day?
- What does my home feel like?
- What does a perfect weekday look like? A weekend?
- How am I growing, contributing, and enjoying life?
- What's bringing me joy and purpose?

This is the life where you stay the course, and everything works out well. It's comforting, it's familiar, but hopefully, also fulfilling.

# LIFE #2
## If Everything Changed Tomorrow

Now imagine that your current life disappears. Your career or industry vanishes, poof. For example, in my case, imagine that restaurants were suddenly no longer a thing. You can't go back to what you know. You have to reinvent.

This is the life that asks: What else could I be?
Ask yourself:

- What else am I interested in, but haven't explored?
- If I had to start from scratch, where would I begin?
- What hidden skills or passions could I finally put to use?
- What industries or spaces excite me?
- What kind of people would I surround myself with?
- What lifestyle would support this version of me?

This life may feel uncomfortable at first, but it's full of creative potential. It opens doors you didn't even know you were allowed to walk through.

# LIFE #3
## If Nothing Held You Back

Now, let go of all limits.

Time, money, age, location, family, status, none of it is an issue. Nobody would laugh. Nobody would question you. And everything is possible.

What would you do if nothing stood in your way?

Ask yourself:

- What would I do purely for joy or meaning?
- What would I spend my days doing?
- Where in the world would I be?
- Would I create something? Teach something? Travel? Perform? Build?
- What would give me energy every single day?

This life helps you tap into your unfiltered desires, the ones that get buried under guilt, responsibility, or fear. It may be surprising, even silly, or feel out of character. That's okay. That's the point. Write it anyway.

# STEP 3
## Reflect on the Patterns and Surprises

Now that you have your three lives sketched out, it's time to reflect.

Look at what shows up more than once. Is there a recurring theme? A thread of impact, creativity, freedom, connection, or adventure?

Look at what surprises you. Maybe you wrote about something you haven't thought about in years. Maybe you uncovered a desire you'd been quietly ignoring.

Ask yourself:

- Which life feels the most me?
- Which life feels most exciting or energizing?
- Which life scares me in a good way?
- Which elements from each version do I want to start incorporating now?

You might realize:

- That your "perfect" current path is no longer as exciting as you thought.
- That Life 2 revealed a new skill you're ready to develop.
- That Life 3 uncovered a long-lost dream that still wants your attention.

The beauty here is: you're not choosing just one.

You're designing your real life using parts from all three.

# STEP 4
## You Only Have One Life; Design It with Intention

Here's the final truth that brings this exercise home:
You only have one life. And you don't have unlimited time.

So why live in default mode?

So many women live reactively, responding to others' needs, meeting external expectations, waiting for the "right" time. But your best life isn't waiting for permission. It's waiting for clarity. And that clarity comes from designing your future, not guessing or wishing.

When you combine elements of all three lives, you create a version of your future that is not only possible, it's energizing. And from there, you can begin to take small, intentional steps toward it.

You don't need to change everything overnight. But you can:

- Register for that course.
- Block off time for your passion.
- Say yes to the idea you've been sitting on.
- Try something new, outside your comfort zone.
- Begin shifting your calendar, your mindset, your environment.

Designing your life is a process, but it begins with giving yourself permission to imagine more.

You don't need to change everything overnight. But you can:

- Register for that course.
- Block off time for your passion.
- Say yes to the idea you've been sitting on.
- Try something new, outside your comfort zone.
- Begin shifting your calendar, your mindset, your environment.

Designing your life is a process, but it begins with giving yourself permission to imagine more.

 # YOUR LIFE DESIGN CHECKLIST

Here's a simple checklist to walk through this exercise. Take 30 to 60 minutes of quiet time. You can also repeat this every few years as your life evolves.

1.  Write your Life #1 (perfect version of your current path)

    ☐ Describe your ideal workday, home life, relationships, lifestyle

    ☐ Be detailed: what are you doing, where are you, who are you with?

2.  Write your Life #2 (if your career disappeared)

    ☐ Explore what new directions you'd consider if starting fresh

    ☐ Get creative; what else could you be, do, create?

3.  Write your Life #3 (no limits life)

    ☐ Remove all barriers; money, time, status

    ☐ Let your imagination run wild. Be bold.

4.  Look for patterns

    ☐ What themes repeat across all three?

    ☐ What values or desires are most consistent?

5.  Identify surprises

    ☐ What ideas or dreams came up that you weren't expecting?

    ☐ What felt exciting or "alive" on the page?

6.  Highlight your must-haves

    ☐ What do you want to integrate into your real life now?
    ☐ Choose 2–3 small steps you can take in the next 30 days

7.  Revisit this process every 6 months

    ☐ Your life changes. Your goals will evolve. That's normal.
    ☐ Use this tool to stay grounded, intentional, and inspired.

This is how you stop living on autopilot.
This is how you step out of comparison.
This is how you build your life, not someone else's.

Up next, we'll use one of my favourite tools: The Wheel of Life.

Once you've defined the big picture for life, you'll need the right tools to protect it.

Let's move forward.

# CHRISTINE'S LIFE DESIGN; A PERSONAL EXAMPLE

To help bring this concept to life, I want to share my own experience with the Design Your Life exercise. I did this for the first time during a workshop at Stanford, and I still return to it regularly as a compass for aligning my choices with my vision.

At the time, I was married, with two wonderful daughters. Dunkin' Donuts Lebanon was growing steadily, we had around 20 stores. Semsom, our brand spreading Lebanese cuisine with a twist, was in multiple countries, and I felt I was on a solid path. But the exercise challenged me to stretch beyond my day-to-day reality and dream up not just one, but three versions of my future.

# LIFE 1
## My Ideal Path

In this version, I built on the life I was already living. I saw myself expanding my F&B business to 40 stores, doubling its size, and I wanted Semsom to get to 20 years, it was 3 years back then. I envisioned a thriving business, a happy family life, traveling regularly with my husband and daughters, and financial freedom that would allow me to enjoy the journey without money being a concern.

It was a natural, evolved extension of what I had; the "perfect" version of my current trajectory.

# LIFE 2
## The Reinvention Path

Then came the curveball: What if my current industry disappeared entirely? What if restaurants no longer existed?

That's when I thought: I would dedicate myself to mentoring female entrepreneurs. I had always found joy in supporting others, helping women unlock their potential and navigate their business journeys. This alternate path felt deeply fulfilling and impactful.

This became the seed of what would later grow into The Empowering Tribe, Her Book Club, the Spark Program, and the Catalyst of Growth Corporate Workshops.

## LIFE 3
**The Wild Dream**

Now for the fun one. If time and money were not an issue, and no one would laugh, what would I do?

Easy. I'd be a travel blogger.

I'd explore every corner of the world, immerse myself in new cultures, and share my experiences along the way. Back then, I had visited around 30 or 40 countries, and I set a bold goal: reach 100 countries and tell the stories of those adventures.

# ONE LIFE, THREE DREAMS

The facilitator then said something that shook me:
"You only have one life. You don't get to live all three. But you can design one life that includes pieces of all three."

So I asked myself: How do I integrate these three versions into one happy, meaningful life?

And that's exactly what I did.

- Still growing and expanding our F&B ventures. Dunkin is at 40 stores and Semsom is 17 years old.
- Mentoring thousands of women through leadership programs and workshops.
- At 81 countries; still working toward my 100 country goal.
- Sharing my travels and reflections on social media and in this book.

I didn't wait. I didn't assume I had endless time.

I chose to say yes, to myself, to my values, and to the life I wanted.

# YOUR TURN

You'll find the Design Your Life worksheet on the QR code below. I encourage you to take this seriously. Block 30 to 60 minutes. Do it alone, without distractions.

- Map out your ideal life (based on what you have now).
- Create an alternate life (if your career vanished tomorrow).
- Design your dream life (if time, money, or opinions didn't matter).

Then look for the threads. What ideas, dreams, or values show up across all three?

Those are your guiding lights.

And once you see them clearly, make a plan to weave them into your actual life; one brave, intentional step at a time.

Because this is your one wild, precious life. Make it yours.

# DEFINE YOUR HAPPY, MEANINGFUL LIFE

Now that you've tried the 3 life excercise, the question becomes:

**So what do you want?**

Before you build a career plan, scale a business, or make your next big decision, you need to get clear on something more fundamental:

What does a **happy, meaningful life** look like *for* you?

This may sound simple, but in reality, most of us are chasing goals we never stopped to define. We're responding to expectations; family, culture, social media, corporate systems; rather than choosing with intention.

The first and most powerful step to real alignment is deciding what success and happiness actually mean to you, across all areas of life, not just your career.

# THE WHEEL OF LIFE

For the past five years, I've used a simple but transformative tool with the women I mentor: the **Wheel of Life.**

I wish I had discovered it earlier. It's a structured, visual way to reflect on all the dimensions of your life; not just work, but also family, health, love, personal growth, money, and more. It forces you to zoom out and look at the whole picture.

Most women are making big career decisions while only looking at one slice of their life. The Wheel helps you pause and assess the full pie; so you can decide which areas are strong, which ones need attention, and most importantly: *what matters most to you right now.*

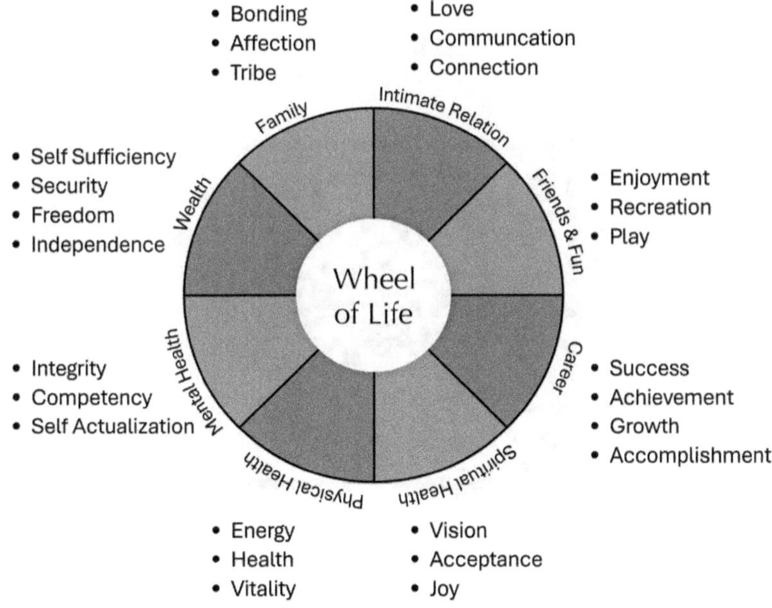

Here's how it works:

1. **Rate each area of your life** on a scale from 0 to 10. Think honestly; how satisfied are you right now in this area?
2. **Reflect:** What do your scores reveal? Where are you thriving? Where do you feel drained?
3. **Choose 2–3 focus areas** for the next six months; based not just on the lowest scores, but on what feels most important to you at this season.
4. **Set meaningful, specific goals** in those focus areas; and create action steps to move forward.
5. **Track your progress weekly,** and review your Wheel again every six months.

(A full version of this exercise is available on our website. I encourage you to print it or use it digitally and revisit it often.)

# YOUR PRIORITIES WILL CHANGE. THAT'S NOT FAILURE, THAT'S GROWTH

Here's one of the most important things to understand about the Wheel: **it's a moving target.**

The priorities you had at 22 will likely not be the same at 32, 42, or 52, and that's not only normal, it's healthy. What matters is that you're checking in with yourself regularly.

Want to sprint in your career in your 30s and slow down in your 40s? Great.

Want to pause for a few years to raise your kids and come back strong later? Totally valid.

Follow your passion and travel the world? Why not?

Want to pivot industries or start something brand new in midlife? Yes, please.

The only "wrong" choice is the one you make unconsciously, driven by guilt, fear, or pressure.

Use the Wheel of Life to get clear on what matters to you, and then choose your next steps based on that clarity, not external noise.

Because when your life is designed around your true values, that's where peace and power meet.

And that's when you begin to say yes; not out of obligation, but out of alignment.

---

# THE POWER OF A VISION BOARD

Let's talk about vision boards.

Some people love them. Some don't. I happen to be one of the ones who do, and I've found them to be not just inspiring, but magical.

Every year, once I've done my Wheel of Life exercise and outlined the goals and dreams I want to pursue across different areas: health, relationships, career, finances, personal growth, and more. I take those reflections and turn them into something visual. That's when the vision board comes in.

It's become a beautiful tradition in my family. During the Christmas break, my daughters and I sit down together to reflect on the past year and dream into the next one. We go through each area of our lives, just like on the Wheel of Life, and choose a few key goals, dreams, or intentions. Some are for the coming year. Others might be long-term aspirations that stay on the board for several years. That's okay. It's not about deadlines, it's about direction.

We then gather photos, words, symbols, and images that represent those dreams. Some years we print them out and create a physical board to hang above our desks. Other years, we create digital vision boards and set them as wallpapers on our phones or laptops. The key is to keep your vision visible, somewhere you can glance at it regularly and be reminded of what matters most.

And here's the part that gives me goosebumps: 90% of what I've put on my vision board... actually happened. My daughter calls it "the magic board". I don't think it's magic in the fantasy sense, I believe it's the power of intention, focus and action. When you set a vision and revisit it often, your mind starts working toward it. Your actions align. And somehow, the creator (or the universe) meets you halfway.

If you've never tried a vision board before, why not give it a shot? It's a fun, creative, and surprisingly powerful tool to reconnect with your dreams. Do it solo with a cup of coffee and some quiet music. Or turn it into a playful evening with your friends, your partner, or your kids. Let it be a space to dream big.

And if you want to take it further, check out the 2026 Power to Say Yes Planner. Inside, you'll find dedicated space for your vision board, along with tools like the Wheel of Life, the Eisenhower Box, monthly check-ins, and more, everything we talked about in this book, translated into an easy-to-use format so you can live it every day.

Because dreaming is powerful. But dreaming with intention? That's where the magic happens.

Remember: this isn't about perfection, it's about direction. Let your vision board be a mirror of your joy, your purpose, and your possibilities.

All the excercises in the book are available for you to try.

All you have to do it to scan this QR code and get all the workbooks.

Try them, it improved my life, I hope it will improve yours too.

PART 3
LIVING IT
OUT

# BOUNDARIES ARE A SKILLSET; PROTECTING THE LIFE YOU DESIGNED

# YOU'VE DONE THE WORK.

You've reflected on what matters. You've clarified your vision. You've designed a life that aligns with your energy, your values, your priorities.

But there's one critical truth we need to face:

> **A beautiful life design means nothing if you don't protect it.**

The book is called *The Power to Say Yes!* Yes to your happy, meaningful life.

And the truth is; the best way to say yes is **by learning how to say no.**

That's where **boundaries** come in.

Boundaries are not harsh walls or rigid rules. They are loving guardrails that preserve the space you've intentionally created. They're how you defend your energy, protect your time, and make your priorities more than just good intentions.

Without boundaries, your vision stays a wish. With boundaries, **it becomes a lifestyle.**

And here's the good news: boundaries are a skillset. You're not born with it, you learn it, you practice it, and eventually, it becomes second nature.

# WHY BOUNDARIES ARE ESPECIALLY IMPORTANT FOR WOMEN

For many women, setting boundaries can feel unnatural or even selfish. We're raised to nurture, to please, to accommodate. Many of us were taught that being "a good girl" means being flexible, available, agreeable. And that makes boundary-setting feel like conflict, or worse, rejection.

But here's the truth:

Boundaries are not rejection. They are clarity.

They let others know what's okay and what's not, without guilt, without drama.

You are not selfish for protecting your energy.

You are not cold for protecting your peace.

You are not difficult for asking for what you need.

You are a woman with vision, and boundaries are how you honor that vision.

# BOUNDARIES START WITH THE WHEEL OF LIFE

Let's go back to the Wheel of Life. You've identified your top priorities for the next six months. Let's say they are:

- Health
- Wealth
- Family

Each of these priorities will require space, time, energy, and intention. Boundaries are the tools that make room for these.

Let's look at each one in depth.

# HEALTH: BOUNDARIES AROUND YOUR BODY AND ENERGY

If you've chosen health as a priority, whether it's fitness, nutrition, sleep, mental health, or navigating hormonal changes, this needs to be reflected in your schedule and conversations.

Boundary Examples:

- "I go to the gym Monday, Wednesday, and Friday from 8 to 9am. I'm not available during that time."
- "I stop eating after 8pm to follow my fasting protocol."
- "I no longer take meetings before 9am; that's my wellness window."

If you're married or living with a partner, involve them:

"This is what I'm focusing on right now. I'll need your support with the kids during this time. It's important for me."

If you work with a boss or team:

"I'd like to shift my availability slightly. I'm making health a priority, and it helps me show up stronger during the day."

Note: You don't need to over-explain. State your needs clearly and respectfully. If you treat your boundary like a non-negotiable, others will too.

# WEALTH: BOUNDARIES AROUND MONEY, EARNING, AND TIME

Wealth as a priority could mean increasing your income, launching a side hustle, building financial literacy, or beginning to invest. But none of these happen by accident, they require time and attention.

Boundary Examples:

- "I've blocked out Thursday evenings for my side project."

- "I no longer lend money to friends or family without a clear plan."
- 
- "I'm learning about investing, so I've committed 30 minutes every weekend to financial education."

You might also need to ask:

- Could I renegotiate my role or raise?
- Am I spending in alignment with my values?
- What do I need to stop saying yes to in order to earn more or invest smarter?

Some learnings:

Start investing early, I started late, but now I've taught my daughters to begin while they're young. The earlier you start, the more freedom you'll create.

This is also a great boundary to teach your future self:

"I will protect a portion of my income to build long-term security."

# FAMILY: BOUNDARIES WITH THE PEOPLE YOU LOVE MOST

This is often the hardest area to set boundaries, because it involves the people we're closest to.

But clarity doesn't harm relationships, it strengthens them.

Family boundaries can help you:

- Be present with your children
- Protect intimacy in your partnership
- Avoid burnout as a caregiver
- Navigate expectations from extended family

Boundary Examples:

- "I don't respond to work emails after 6pm, that's family time."
- "I need 20 minutes to decompress after work before I re-engage at home."
- "I won't attend every family event, I'll choose what feels aligned."

Do this as a couple:

Sit down with your partner every few months. Use the Wheel of Life together. Ask:

- What are your top 3 priorities?
- What are mine?
- What boundaries do we need to support each other?

Without alignment, resentment builds. With alignment, you become a team.

# HOW TO ACTUALLY SET BOUNDARIES; STEP BY STEP

Drawing from authors like Brené Brown, Nedra Glover Tawwab, and coaching psychology, here's a practical guide to setting and holding boundaries:

## STEP 1
### Know What You Want

If you don't know what matters most to you, your boundaries will always be vague or reactionary. This is why the Wheel of Life is your starting point.

## STEP 2
### Name It Clearly

Say what you need without apology or overexplanation. Clarity is kindness.

Examples:

- "I'm not available after 6pm; that's my time for family and rest."
- "I'm working on a side project, so I'm protecting two evenings a week for that."
- "I'm not going to attend that event; I need some downtime this weekend."

You're not being rude. You're being responsible; for your own well-being.

## STEP 3
**Enforce It Calmly**

Expect pushback. Some people are used to your old patterns. Stay calm, and repeat the boundary instead of defending it.

Example:

- "I know we used to do things differently, but I've made a change to prioritize [X]. I hope you'll support me."

## STEP 4
**Reassess and Reset Often**

Life changes. So do boundaries. What worked six months ago might not work now. Revisit your priorities. Adjust your calendar. Renegotiate your expectations, with others and yourself.

Scripts for Common Boundary Conversations

**With your boss:**

"I'm currently focusing on both my performance and personal health. I'd like to schedule my gym time in the morning, so I'll be available after 9am on weekdays. I'm confident this won't impact my output, in fact, it improves it."

**With your partner:**

"I've realized I need quiet time in the morning before I jump into family or work. Could we create a 30-minute solo buffer for each of us every day?"

**With extended family:**

"I appreciate the invitation, but we've committed to keeping weekends slower for the kids this month. Thanks for understanding, let's find another time soon."

# YOUR BOUNDARY BLUEPRINT

Use this journaling prompt to define and declare your own:

1.      My top 3 priorities this season:

   1. ______________________________________________
   2. ______________________________________________
   3. ______________________________________________

2.      For each, write:
   1.   What does success look like?
   2.   What gets in the way?
   3.   What boundary do I need?

3.      This week, I will:

   1.   Set this one boundary: ____________________
   2.   Communicate it to: ______________________
   3.   Protect it by: __________________________

## Final Thoughts: Boundaries = Freedom

There's a myth that boundaries are restrictive. But the truth is; they're liberating.
When you protect what matters, you:

- Work with more focus
- Rest without guilt
- Show up fully with loved ones
- Honor your time, your body, and your vision

**"You can't say yes to the life you want until you start saying no to the things that don't serve it."**

So speak up. Block the time. Have the talk. Set the line.

You've done the hard work of designing a beautiful life.

Now it's time to protect it; fiercely, unapologetically, and with love.

---

# WHAT ABOUT MEN?

In a book dedicated to women reclaiming their power, it's only fair, and essential, to talk about the men in our lives. Because men matter. Fathers, brothers, partners, friends, colleagues, men make up half the world's population, and many of them are our fiercest supporters.

I, for one, could not have done everything I've done without the amazing men around me. From the men in my family, my father and brothers, to the chosen men in my life; my special person, YPO friends, my forum buddies, and colleagues; they've been by my side cheering me on, celebrating my wins, and lifting me through the harder moments.

# TWO KEY SHIFTS IN MEN

Over the years, I've noticed a significant shift in how men engage with the women around them, especially in the professional space. As someone who leads leadership workshops for women in corporates, I've been pleasantly surprised by the rising number of requests from men asking: Can you do a session for us, too? We want to better understand how to support the women on our teams.

Here are the two shifts I've observed:

## 1. Men Want to Help, But Don't Always Know How

In a recent panel with over 160 participants, 60 of whom were men, it was the men who asked the most questions. The common thread: How can we support?

The answer is simple, but not always easy: listen, learn, and don't judge. Have the courageous conversations. For example, if a team member is about to take maternity leave, ask her: What do you want your return to look like? If she wants to fully disconnect for those months and focus on her baby, honor that. If she's hoping to stay connected and still eyeing the next promotion, support that too, with clear expectations.

The point isn't to assume, it's to ask, and to listen without judgment without making her feel like a failure if she doesn't choose the straight line path. When we allow women to define what success looks like for themselves in each season, without penalizing them, we create truly inclusive workplaces.

**2. Men Want the Power to Say Yes, Too**

The second shift is even more exciting: many men now want the same **power to say yes** to their version of a happy, meaningful life. I've seen fathers prioritize family over fast-tracking their careers. I've seen partners set boundaries at work to be more present at home. These are not exceptions anymore, they're part of a quiet but steady revolution.

And we need to support them, just as we ask them to support us.

# WHEN MEN ARE NOT SUPPORTIVE

Of course, this is not always the case. Some of you reading this may be surrounded by unsupportive men, or even worse, by bullies who try to control, belittle, or limit you. If that's your reality, know this: you are not alone, and you still have choices.

This is where the work begins: setting boundaries, protecting your peace, and finding your power. Therapy, coaching, or simply confiding in someone you trust can help you get there. And community, whether it's friends, mentors, or platforms like The Empowering Tribe or Her Book Club, can make all the difference.

If the people closest to you aren't lifting you, seek support elsewhere. Find people who believe in you, who see your potential, and who remind you that your dreams are valid. We all deserve that kind of support.

And finally, no matter who's around you, don't fall into the victim mindset. Choose accountability. Choose action. Even if the step is small, take it. I've seen countless women break free from limiting environments and rebuild lives on their own terms. You can too.

# WHY TIME IS YOUR MOST PRECIOUS ASSET

You can always earn more money. You can never earn more time.

This simple truth is often ignored in the chaos of everyday life. But when you truly understand it, when you feel it deep in your bones, it becomes a guiding principle. Because time isn't neutral. It's your most precious, non-renewable, and irreplaceable asset.

And yet, so many women spend their days in reaction mode rather than intention. We juggle endless obligations. We absorb the invisible emotional load. We say yes to things out of guilt, fear, or duty, rather than clarity or choice. And somewhere in all that busy-ness, we lose touch with ourselves, our vision, and our happiness.

So let me say this clearly and boldly: **If you want to live a happy, meaningful, and intentional life, you must learn to protect your time like the treasure it is.**

# TIME IS THE FOUNDATION OF EVERYTHING ELSE

Time is the structure on which your entire life is built. It is the canvas on which you paint your relationships, your career, your family, your dreams. Every aspiration, habit, connection, and goal lives and dies by how you spend your hours and your energy.

If you want to:

- Improve your health → you need time to rest, move, breathe, and nourish yourself.
- Grow your wealth → you need time to think, learn, create, invest, and take risks.
- Raise thriving, connected children → you need time to be present, attentive, and loving.
- Have a nurturing romantic relationship → you need time to connect, talk, and simply be together.
- Feed your spiritual life, your creativity, your joy → you need time to unplug and reflect.

No app, no tool, no external hack will ever give you that. It starts with you claiming your time as yours.

# FROM AWARENESS TO ACTION

You can't change what you don't measure. And you can't improve your time if you don't know where it's going. So the first step is awareness.

Try this: for the next 3 to 5 days, keep a time log.

- Write down everything you do, hour by hour.
- Include the small things: emails, scrolling, errands, chatting, multitasking.
- Don't judge yourself. Just observe.


When you review your log, ask:

- What patterns do I see?
- What gives me energy?
- What drains me?
- What feels aligned with who I want to be and what doesn't?

Most women are shocked by how much time is lost to things that don't really matter. We say we have no time for exercise, reading, sleep, or joy, but spend hours scrolling on Tiktok.

Awareness is the first courageous step toward reclaiming your power.

# THE WEEKLY PLANNING RITUAL

One of the most powerful habits you can build is a weekly planning ritual. Just 30 minutes once a week can transform your schedule, your stress levels, and your results.

Choose a quiet time. Sunday evening, Monday morning, or whatever fits your rhythm.

Here's your checklist:

- Review your Wheel of Life priorities and top focus areas
- Write down your top 3 goals for the week
- Block out your non-negotiables (workouts, sleep, date night, family dinner, fun activity)
- Schedule deep work blocks for meaningful tasks
- Leave buffer time for rest, breathing room, and catching up
- Review meetings, errands, and obligations → cancel or delegate what drains you

Show me your calendar and I'll show you

If your schedule is only full of everyone else's demands, where is your own life supposed to fit?

And if you want to take it further, check out the **2026 Power to Say Yes Planner.** Inside, you'll find dedicated space for your monthly, weekly check-ins, and more, everything we talked about in this book, translated into an easy-to-use format so you can live it every day.

# WHAT GETS SCHEDULED, GETS DONE

You might have big dreams. But unless they exist on your calendar, they exist only in your imagination.

- Use time blocking to protect focus hours. Treat these like sacred appointments.
- Build in deep work sessions without interruption.
- Try using the Eisenhower Matrix to sort between what's urgent and what's important.
- Don't over-plan. Give yourself space to breathe, adapt, and be human.

The goal is not to be busy. The goal is to be aligned with your values and vision.

# THE POWER OF THE EISENHOWER BOX: MASTERING YOUR TIME WITH INTENTION

One of the simplest yet most powerful time management tools I use, daily, weekly, and monthly, is the Eisenhower Matrix, also known as the Urgent-Important Box. It's a visual system that helps you decide what truly deserves your attention, what can be planned, what should be delegated, and what can simply be dropped.

The idea is straightforward: every task belongs in one of four quadrants based on its level of urgency and importance. It's deceptively simple and profoundly effective.

## Eisenhower Box

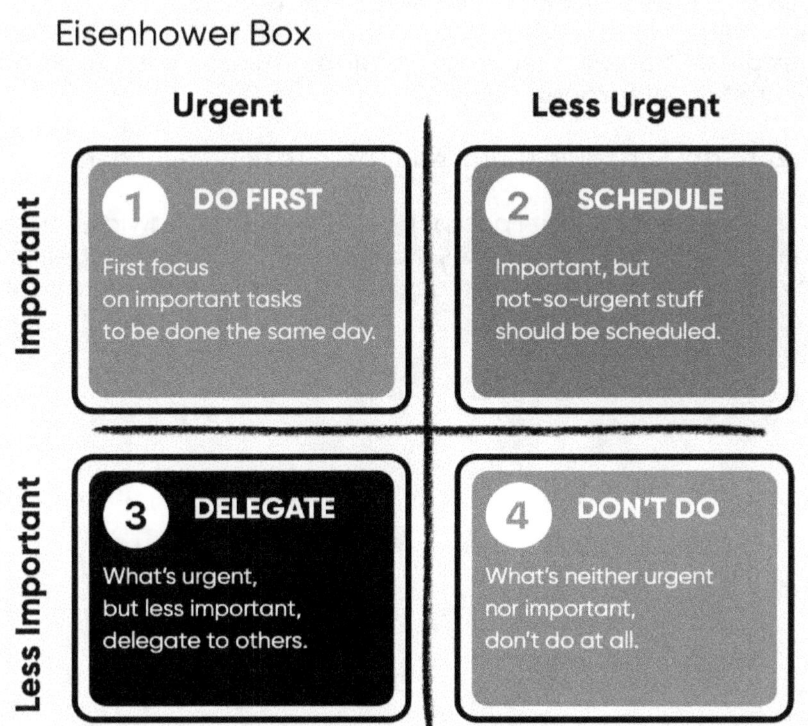

# QUADRANT 1
**Urgent & Important**

These are the tasks that require immediate attention and have significant consequences if left undone. They often involve deadlines, emergencies, or crises.
Example: A key project deadline, a medical emergency, a last-minute board presentation.

**What to do:** Start here. Tackle these tasks first.

# QUADRANT 2
**Important but Not Urgent**

This is where transformation happens. These are the long-term vision tasks, the ones that build your business, your health, your relationships. The only reason they're not done more often is because they don't scream for your attention.

**Examples:** Strategic planning, working out, time with loved ones, personal development.

**What to do:** Schedule them. Add them to your calendar.

I have a personal rule: if I postpone this kind of task twice, the third time, I must do it, no excuses. I call these the grasshopper tasks, they keep hopping from one day to the next until we take control.

# QUADRANT 3
**Urgent but Not Important**

These are tasks that appear urgent but don't really move your life forward. They often come from other people's priorities.

**Examples:** Some emails, interruptions, meeting requests, last-minute "urgent" asks that aren't really aligned with your goals.

**What to do:** Delegate.

Become the queen of delegation. This quadrant is a trap. The more time you spend here, the less energy you have for what truly matters.

# QUADRANT 4
**Not Urgent & Not Important**

This is where time quietly disappears. These tasks do not serve your goals and aren't urgent either.

**Examples:** Endless scrolling, watching mindless content, unnecessary meetings.

**What to do:** Eliminate. Let them go without guilt.

# HOW TO USE IT

Whether you're planning your day, your week, or your month, do a full brain dump of everything on your plate. Then classify each item into one of the four quadrants. Once your tasks are sorted:

1. Start with Quadrant 1.
2. Schedule Quadrant 2 with intention.
3. Delegate Quadrant 3.
4. Eliminate Quadrant 4.

If you use this tool consistently, your entire mindset around time will shift. You'll stop reacting and start leading. You'll spend more energy on what matters instead of just what's shouting the loudest.

Remember: success is built in Quadrant 2; where urgency doesn't pressure you, but importance drives you.

# AUDIT YOUR TIME LIKE YOU AUDIT YOUR FINANCES

Imagine handing out $100 bills to anyone who asked, without thinking.

You wouldn't do that with your money.

So why do we give away our time so freely?

We give hours to:

- Meetings we didn't need to attend
- Social media we didn't mean to scroll
- Conversations that drain us
- Obligations that don't reflect our heart

What if you asked, every time:

- Is this aligned with my highest priorities?
- Is this something I truly want to say yes to?
- Is this energizing or depleting?

If the answer is no, it's a boundary moment.

**And remember:** every time you say no to the wrong thing, you're saying yes to the right thing.

# YOU ONLY GET ONE LIFE

This is bigger than scheduling. This is about agency. About creating a life that reflects who you are.

You have one life. One story. One chance to make it meaningful.

This isn't about hustle. It's not about squeezing in more. It's about choosing what matters most, and honoring it with your time, your presence, and your energy.

So take the time to:

- Reflect with honesty
- Plan with intention
- Say yes with your whole heart
- Say no with clarity and kindness

Protect what matters most.

Because your time is not neutral.

It is sacred. It is fleeting. It is yours.

And when you begin to treat it that way, everything else begins to align.

# WHAT ABOUT HAVING FUN?

When you're designing your happy, meaningful life, there's one element that often gets left behind; fun. We talk so much about career, strategy, parenting, health, and financial planning… but what about joy? What about spontaneity? What about pure, unproductive fun?

It's easy to get swept into the seriousness of life, especially when we're juggling roles, responsibilities, and expectations. But here's the truth: a well-designed life must include joy, laughter, and freedom.
Life isn't meant to be a checklist of goals. It's meant to be lived. And part of living fully is giving yourself permission to play, to rest, to chill.

So when you're planning your life, remember to intentionally schedule:

· Time with friends that energize you
· Travel and new experiences
· Long walks with no agenda
· Books, movies, music, or art that light you up
· Yoga retreats or dance classes, or whatever makes you feel alive
· Days where nothing is planned and you just follow the flow

Design a life that's worth living, not just surviving.

The same applies to your budget. Over the years, I've seen both extremes, some people who are so focused on saving and investing that they forget to enjoy their life... and others who are so in-the-moment that they forget to prepare for the future, for retirement, or for their children's education.

The goal is balance. Here's how I personally approach this, and it's made all the difference in how I feel about both my finances and my freedom:

1. First, a fixed portion of my income goes straight to investments.

2. Second, I cover essential fixed costs; especially anything related to my daughters (now at university), rent, and day-to-day living.

3. Third, I allocate 10% of my income to guilt-free pleasures. Yes, you read that right: 10% purely for fun, no guilt allowed.

So whether it's your time or your money, remember to invest a little of both in truly enjoying life. It's easy to get caught up in responsibilities, but creating space for joy and fulfillment is just as essential to your overall well-being.

Next, we're diving into something equally important: Your energy, how you manage it, protect it, and use it to create the life you want.

# ENERGY MANAGEMENT; YOUR SECRET SUPERPOWER

If time is your most limited resource, energy is your most renewable one, but only if you know how to manage it well.

I always say: Energy is like a bucket.

Every action, every person, every decision either fills that bucket or drains it.

The key to energy management is awareness. Ask yourself:

- What activities light me up?
- What drains me, even if it only takes 10 minutes?
- What habits replenish me on a physical, emotional, or spiritual level?
- Who in my life brings sunshine, and who brings shadows?

Let's talk about people. I divide them into two simple categories:

**The Sun:** They enter a room and light it up. They energize you, uplift you, and make things feel possible.

**The Moon:** They don't mean harm, but they drain the energy from the room. They often complain, worry, or bring heavy emotional loads.

It's important to know who's who in your life, not to judge, but to set smart boundaries.
If you're already tired, and you get a call from a Moon person, don't answer. Just send a quick message:

"Hey, today is hectic. I'll call you tomorrow."

Then reach out the next day when your tank is full and you have the energy to show up without resentment.
This is your responsibility.

You can't always control who's in your life, but you can control how and when you engage with them.

# THE SANDWICH TECHNIQUE

This is one of my favorite personal strategies, one I developed and continue to share with anyone open to protecting their energy. Every time I know I have something coming up that will drain my energy: a tough meeting, a long admin task, an emotionally charged conversation, I plan to sandwich it between two things that boost my energy.

Example:

- Morning workout
- Admin review
- Lunch with a friend

This way, you walk through the day in balance. You don't wait for burnout. You design your energy flow.

# WEEKLY PLANNING: NOT JUST TIME, BUT ENERGY

Every Sunday, I sit down and plan my week, not just in terms of tasks, but in terms of energy.

Where are the high-impact moments? Where do I need to recharge? Where do I need protection from emotional vampires?

This practice makes all the difference. You'll find that life doesn't feel so overwhelming when your week is shaped intentionally, with your time and your energy in mind.

# FINAL NOTE

You don't need to be superwoman. You just need to know how to protect your most precious resources: your time and your energy.

When you do that, consistently and unapologetically, you become unstoppable; not because you're doing more, but because you're doing what matters in a way that feels powerful, grounded, and deeply you.

# TIME MANAGEMENT WORKSHEET

1. Top 3 Priorities This Month (from Wheel of Life)

- ☐ ______________________________
- ☐ ______________________________
- ☐ ______________________________

2. Time Blocking Plan

- ☐ What non-negotiable time blocks can I reserve for these priorities?
- ☐ What tasks or meetings can be delegated, postponed, or removed?

3. My Ideal Weekly Routine Snapshot

- ☐ Morning Rituals:
- ☐ Workouts:
- ☐ Work Focus Hours:
- ☐ Recovery Time:
- ☐ Family/Connection:
- ☐ Evening Routine:

4. My Weekly "Not To Do" List:

______________________________

______________________________

______________________________

______________________________

______________________________

______________________________

# ENERGY MANAGEMENT WORKSHEET

1.  Energy Givers (List 5 things or people that boost your energy)

    - _______________________________________________
    - _______________________________________________
    - _______________________________________________
    - _______________________________________________
    - _______________________________________________

2.  Energy Drainers (List 5 things or people that deplete your energy):

    - _______________________________________________
    - _______________________________________________
    - _______________________________________________
    - _______________________________________________
    - _______________________________________________

3. Sun vs. Moon People

    - Who are the "Suns" in your life? How can you spend more time with them?
    - Who are the "Moons"? When do you need to protect your energy?

4. Sandwich Strategy for the Week

    - Draining Task: _________________________
    - Energy Boost Before: ___________________
    - Energy Boost After: ____________________

5. Weekly Energy Plan

    - What rituals will I use to stay energized? (Movement, rest, nature, connection, etc.)
    - How will I protect my high-energy time zones?

Repeat these practices weekly to maintain balance, alignment, and power in how you show up for your life.

# HAPPINESS IN THE SECOND HALF OF LIFE

(The Taboo We Need to Talk About More)

Let's talk about something that doesn't get enough attention, yet it affects every woman: the second half of life, and particularly the perimenopause and menopause years. This phase, often beginning around age 35 and stretching well into our 50s and beyond, is a profound period of transition, biologically, emotionally, and spiritually. And yet, most of us are not prepared for it.

We're told how to thrive in our 20s. We're coached on career moves in our 30s. But what about when your hormones shift, your brain rewires, your energy fluctuates, and suddenly, the strategies that worked before no longer serve you?

## THE SHIFT IN INTELLIGENCE

One of the most eye-opening books I've read on this topic is **From Strength to Strength** by Professor Arthur Brooks. He explains how we move from fluid intelligence; the ability to solve new problems quickly, often peaking in our 30s, to crystallized intelligence, which grows as we age and is built on wisdom, insight, pattern recognition, and mentoring others.

So if you try to replicate your 30s in your 50s, you'll often end up frustrated and unhappy. Instead, the key is to pivot, to embrace the new form of intelligence and power that comes with age. This is the age of legacy, influence, and depth. It's about shifting your identity from doer to guide, from driver to visionary. I strongly recommend reading this book to plan your happy, meaningful life for the second half of your life.

# **UNDERSTANDING PERIMENOPAUSE AND MENOPAUSE**

Let's demystify the biological part.

Perimenopause can start as early as age 35 and typically lasts up to 10 years before menopause officially begins, which is defined as 12 consecutive months without a menstrual period.

This means many of us are navigating this transition while still in the middle of our careers, raising kids, or even launching new businesses. And yet, most of the symptoms we experience are dismissed, misdiagnosed, or internalized as personal failures.

There are over 70 documented symptoms of perimenopause, from mood swings and hot flashes to brain fog, anxiety, sleep disruption, joint pain, and more.

And these symptoms can affect your life in very real ways.

- When you're sitting in a boardroom and forget your words; it hits your confidence.
- When you're leading a workshop and a sudden hot flash overtakes you; it rattles your presence.
- When you're juggling brain fog, night sweats, or rage you don't understand; it can shake your identity.

But here's what we need to remember:

This isn't weakness. This is biology. And there are solutions.

From hormone replacement therapy (HRT) to lifestyle shifts, supplements, movement, and mindfulness practices, there are real, science-backed ways to thrive through this phase. The key is awareness.

# YOUR BODY, YOUR POWER

Take ownership:

- Track your cycle (even if it's irregular).
- Get your hormones tested regularly.
- Work with a gynecologist who understands menopause and can offer a range of options.
- Explore resources or join our Empowering

Tribe workshops or Her Book Club sessions, where we openly talk about these changes.

I read that during perimenopause, women face significantly elevated rates of depression, up to 40% higher than before menopause, and are more likely to experience suicidal thoughts or behaviors. And 'gray divorce' (divorce after age 50) has surged, with around 73% of women reporting that menopause or perimenopause played a contributing role.

It's not because women are falling apart, it's because we're going through a profound transformation without a map or support system.

We are not meant to suffer in silence.

We are meant to evolve, boldly, intentionally, and with support.

The truth is, menopause is not the end. It's a rebirth.

# THRIVING IN YOUR 50s (AND BEYOND)

Personally, I can say that my 50s so far have been amazing (I am 51 when writing this book). But they didn't happen by chance. They happened because I took charge.

Here's what's been key for me, and could be for you:

- Building muscle: It's one of the most important ways to support hormone balance and longevity.
- Taking the right supplements: Based on actual deficiencies and guided by lab work.
- Listening to your body: Honoring rest, movement, nourishment, and joy.
- Letting go of outdated definitions of success and embracing what truly matters.
- Surrounding yourself with women on the same path: Join conversations. Find your tribe. Don't walk this alone.

# YOUR HAPPINESS, REDEFINED

This chapter of life is not about decline, it's about redesign.

It's about stepping into your power with more wisdom, more intention, and more alignment than ever before.

And if you're reading this thinking, "Why didn't anyone tell me?", know that you're not alone. That's exactly why I'm writing this. We need more voices talking openly, more women leading boldly, and more communities supporting each other.

You are not broken.

You are not too late.

You are in the exact right season to choose what comes next, and say YES to your second (and maybe best) half.

# THE IN-BETWEEN SEASON

Before we wrap things up, I want to talk about something we don't always name, but we all experience.

The *in*-between season.

That space between who we were and who we're becoming. It's not quite the beginning, not quite the end. Maybe it comes after a big life change: divorce, a career pivot, menopause, burnout, empty nest, or even after reading a book that stirred something inside you.

It can feel uncomfortable, uncertain, sometimes lonely. But it's also where the magic begins.

Because this is the season where you plant the seeds.
That's the beauty of transformation. It rarely happens in straight lines. It unfolds, it circles back, it stretches us gently and sometimes not-so-gently into something new.

You won't have all the answers yet. You may not feel fully ready. But you're asking better questions. You're listening more closely. You're tuning in to what feels good, what feels off, and what's calling you forward.
Try not to rush the in-between.

Let it simmer. Let it shape you.

And when you're ready, the next chapter will be yours to write.

# THE POWER TO SAY YES

So my dear reader, if you've made it to this final part of the book, I'm so proud of you.

Not just because you've reached the last page, but because this means you've taken the first powerful step: choosing to reflect, explore, and take ownership of your life.

This book has been a journey through the different seasons, choices, and emotions that shape a woman's life, from career paths to motherhood, from time and energy management to mindset, boundaries, and self-worth.

We've explored stories of real women, (with revised names) tools like the Wheel of Life, design thinking, and the importance of saying no so we can say yes, with intention and clarity.

You've seen how guilt, limiting beliefs, and the feeling of "not enough" can hold us back, and how awareness, ownership, and community can move us forward.

Now, it's time to step fully into your own version of a happy, meaningful life, on your own terms.

**The power to say yes** is the power to choose.

To choose your path. Your pace. Your definition of success. Your way of working, living, loving, resting, creating.

This is your life. You are not late. You are not too much. You are not behind. You are not a mistake. You are not broken. You are in motion, becoming. Right on time.

And the moment you claim your power to choose; to say yes with intention, and to say no without guilt; you take back authorship of your life.

You no longer outsource your worth. You no longer wait for permission. You begin creating a life that feels aligned with your heart, your values, your vision.

**The power to say yes** is not just about opportunity. It's about ownership.

Ownership of your energy.

Ownership of your voice.

Ownership of your schedule.

Ownership of your story.

So say yes to what lights you up. Yes to boundaries that protect your peace. Yes to rest that nourishes your soul. Yes to growth that excites and stretches you. Yes to presence, to pleasure, to purpose.

And if the voice of doubt shows up, and it will, gently remind it: I'm allowed to design a life I love.

You are not here to please everyone. You are here to live fully. And I warmly invite you to try the exercises shared throughout this book.

They've had a huge impact on my life, and I truly hope they do the same for you. Whether it's the Wheel of Life, or the simple but powerful exercises on time, energy, mindset, or designing your life, give yourself the gift of time to reflect, to experiment, and to listen deeply to what you really want. These tools are here to help you thrive, not just survive. To help you design a life that energizes you, fulfills you, and makes you feel alive.

Download all the worksheets using the QR code

Use the Power of Yes! Planner.

Follow us on Instagram @thecatalystofgrowth

or email us at story@catalystofgrowth.com.

Share your story. Your journey. Your discoveries. Your struggles. Your tiny wins. Our connection doesn't end here.

You hold the pen. This is your life. Say yes.

With love and full belief in your power,

Christine :)

# A HEARTFELT THANK YOU

This book would not have been possible without the extraordinary people who surround me, lift me up, and inspire me every single day.

**To my daughters;** you are the best thing that ever happened to me. You are my greatest teachers, my deepest joy, and one of the biggest reasons I wrote this book. I wanted to capture all the lessons I've learned so that you might walk your 20s with more clarity, ease, and confidence than I ever had. I can't wait to keep cheering you on every step of your journey.

**To my mom, my rock;** none of this would have been possible without you. You were there every afternoon for years, guiding my daughters with love and patience. You gave me the emotional foundation to build everything I am today. Thank you for your unconditional support and constant presence.

**To my dad;** your genes fuel my ambition. Your business sense, your endless creativity (twenty five thousands ideas per minute!), your drive and your energy continue to inspire me. At seventy-eight, you're still traveling the world. My goal is to keep that same fire alive.

**To my siblings;** Philippe, Pierre, Carine; and to Cecilia, Clara and Karim, my sisters/brother-in-law: thank you for being my home team, my steady ground. I know no matter what happens, I have you. In the best and worst of times, your love has been my anchor. And to my beautiful nieces and nephews (Alex, Zaya, Matteo, Sienna, Nady, Luca and hopefully more on the way!), you fill my world with joy.

**To the incredible person in my life;** you've given me something I never knew I needed: grounding. Even though I still fly 1,000 kilometers per hour, when I'm with you, I slow down, I reflect, I breathe. You created the space that helped make this book possible, thank you.

**To my Dunkin' and Semsom teams;** you are the force behind the business I lead. I may be the captain, but without a driven and passionate crew, the ship wouldn't sail. Thank you for putting your heart and soul into everything you do.

**To the Empowering Tribe, the Spark Program, Her Book Club and the Corporate Workshop members;** you inspired so many of the ideas in this book. Through our conversations, our workshops, our mentorship sessions, I've witnessed firsthand the beauty, brilliance, and strength of women stepping into their power. Thank you for letting me be part of your journey.

**To YPO;** a global community that changed my life. From the forums to the Harvard program to the lifelong friendships, you've stood by me in moments of celebration and in moments of struggle. Thank you for the support, the insight, and the impact.

**To my friends;** from childhood to today, you've been the laughter, the wisdom, the soft place to land. Thank you for being there during my divorce, my growth, my chaos, and my calm. You are the family I chose.

**To Mika;** my AI book copywriter, **and Zar,** my book designer; thank you for turning my voice notes, outlines, and thoughts into structure, clarity, and storytelling. This book was better thanks to you.

And finally, **to you, dear reader;** thank you for making it to the final page. I hope this book has touched your heart, sparked your thinking, and helped you move closer to your own happy, meaningful life. I hope it gave you tools, stories, and reminders that you are enough, that you have choices, and that you have **the power to say yes.**

Yes to freedom. Yes to joy. Yes to you.

Until next time,

Sending you lots of love!

# THE POWER TO SAY YES; COMPANION CHECKLISTS

Use these practical checklists to reflect, plan, and realign as you move through your journey. Treat them like a workbook section; come back to them as often as needed.

## Self-Awareness & Understanding Your Options
## Clarity Checklist

☐ Have I reflected on how my life stage is influencing my career right now?

☐ Have I identified any guilt, shame, or limiting beliefs that I want to shift?

☐ Do I believe I have the power to design my life and choose freely?

☐ Have I reviewed other women's journeys and paths for inspiration and clarity?

## Define Your Happy, Meaningful Life
## Wheel of Life Checklist

☐ Have I completed the Wheel of Life with honest ratings for each life area?

☐ Have I identified 2–3 focus areas for the next 6 months?

☐ Have I listed what success looks like for me in those areas?

☐ Have I scheduled a reminder to revisit this exercise in 6 months?

## Life Path Clarity Checklist

- ☐ Which story do I identify with the most (Chris, Nadia, Nour, Rana, Leyla)?

- ☐ What does that path awaken in me; admiration, resistance, excitement?

- ☐ Have I listed what kind of setup or support I'd need for my chosen path?

- ☐ Am I making choices from clarity; not guilt, pressure, or fear?

- ☐ Have I written down what "happy and meaningful" looks like for me, right now?

## Time Ownership Checklist

- ☐ Have I completed a time audit this month to identify drains and time-wasters?

- ☐ Have I designed a weekly plan with space for deep work, focus, and rest?

- ☐ Am I protecting my mornings/evenings with boundaries and rituals?

- ☐ Do I batch similar tasks to reduce mental fatigue and switching?

- ☐ Have I said "no" to at least one thing this week that didn't serve me?

- ☐ Do I end each week with a reset or reflection?

## Energy Awareness & Protection Checklist

☐ Have I tracked what energizes and drains me for a full week?

☐ Do I understand my personal energy rhythm (highs/lows) during the day?

☐ Have I built recovery moments into my daily and weekly flow?

☐ Do I have consistent morning and evening routines that ground me?

☐ Do I regularly practice boundaries; emotional, digital, and physical?

☐ Do I limit exposure to chronic drains (people, habits, environments)?

☐ Am I intentional about protecting high-energy time for high-impact work?

## Ownership & Alignment Checklist

☐ Am I making life choices based on what I truly want?

☐ Have I taken full ownership of at least one major decision recently?

☐ Do I check in with my values regularly (monthly, quarterly)?

☐ Do I speak to myself with kindness and self-compassion?

☐ Have I shared my vision, growth, or struggle with someone I trust?

☐ Have I committed to doing the Wheel of Life every 6 months?

# GLOSSARY

## Accountability

Taking ownership and responsibility for your decisions, actions, and their consequences, without blaming others or external circumstances.

## Alignment

When your values, goals, actions, and energy are all moving in the same direction. Living in alignment means you're not just busy, you're fulfilled.

## Boundaries

The limits you set to protect your time, energy, and mental wellbeing. Boundaries can be physical, emotional, digital, or relational.

## CEO of Your Life

A mindset that encourages you to treat your time, energy, and choices as precious business resources, and to lead with intention and strategy.

## Clarity

The state of being mentally and emotionally clear about what you want, what matters most, and how you want to live.

**Design Your Life (Stanford Method)**

A method developed at Stanford University that uses design thinking to create a joyful, purpose-driven life. It explores multiple life scenarios and encourages creative problem-solving.

**Energy Management**

The practice of noticing and nurturing the things that recharge or drain your energy; and intentionally designing your day around your energy peaks and dips.

**Guilt**

A common but unproductive emotion that many women feel when prioritizing themselves. This book encourages releasing guilt and replacing it with conscious, empowered choices.

**Happy, Meaningful Life**

A personalized vision of what fulfillment looks like to you; one that aligns with your own values, desires, and priorities, not societal expectations.

**Life Operating System**

A personal structure or routine that supports your priorities, helps reduce decision fatigue, and keeps your time and energy aligned with your goals.

**Ownership**

The belief and practice that your life is yours to design. No one else can live it for you. You hold the pen.

**Red Line**

A non-negotiable boundary. Something you commit to upholding because it protects what matters most; whether in your time, values, health, or family life.

## Victim Mindset

A mental state where we believe life is happening to us, rather than for us or through us. It's disempowering. This book encourages shifting from victimhood to agency.

## Agency

The capacity of individuals to have the power and resources to fulfill their potential

## Wheel of Life

A self-assessment tool that helps you visualize key areas of your life (such as career, family, love, health, finances) and rate your satisfaction in each, in order to focus and rebalance.

## Yes

More than agreement, a conscious decision. Saying yes in this book means choosing with clarity, intention, and self-awareness, rather than obligation or fear.

# PERSONAL GROWTH & MINDSET

**The Power to Say Yes** – Christine Assouad

Your very own guide to choosing your path with clarity, ownership, and joy, and living your happy, meaningful life. I had to start with this one;)

**The Happiness Advantage** – Shawn Achor

Based on positive psychology research, this book shows how happiness fuels success, not the other way around, and gives tools to rewire your brain for resilience and joy.

**From Strength to Strength** – Arthur C. Brooks

A must-read for the second half of life. This book explains how our intellectual strengths shift with age, and how to embrace this transition for fulfillment and peace.

**The Mountain Is You** – Brianna Wiest

A powerful book about self-sabotage, emotional resilience, and the process of becoming your highest self by turning your obstacles into your strength.

# RECOMMENDED READING

(And more titles are always being added inside Her Book Club; join us, it's free!)

**The Gifts of Imperfection** – Brené Brown

A compassionate and deeply honest invitation to embrace who you are, let go of who you're supposed to be, and live wholeheartedly.

**Let Them** – Mel Robbins

A simple but liberating mindset shift: let people do what they want, and focus on what you can control. A quick, powerful reminder of boundaries and energy.

**Ikigai: The Japanese Secret to a Long and Happy Life** – Héctor García & Francesc Miralles

Discover the Japanese philosophy of purpose and longevity; aligning passion, mission, vocation, and profession for fulfillment.

# BUSINESS & CAREER

**Start With Why** – Simon Sinek

A powerful framework for building leadership, branding, and purpose. Discover how clarity of "why" leads to lasting impact.

**Never Split the Difference** – Chris Voss

Tactical negotiation tools from a former FBI hostage negotiator that help you influence with empathy in any conversation.
**Crucial Conversations** – Kerry Patterson et al.

Master the art of high-stakes dialogue,in the office, at home, or in conflict. A must-read for better communication.

**Scale Up** – Verne Harnish

An actionable playbook for entrepreneurs and executives to grow and scale their business sustainably.

**Making Big Happen** – Mark Moses

A clear goal-setting and accountability strategy to help you turn bold visions into real-world business success.

**The 4-Hour Workweek** – Tim Ferriss

Rethink the 9 to 5 grind. A provocative blueprint for escaping traditional work models, automating income, and creating freedom.

**Dare to Lead** – Brené Brown

A research-based call for courageous leadership, rooted in vulnerability, clarity of values, and empathy.

**Surrounded by Idiots** – Thomas Erikson

Understand human behavior through the four personality types (red, yellow, green, blue) to enhance communication and teamwork.

# FINANCE & MONEY

**Secrets of the Millionaire Mind** – T. Harv Eker

Explore how your subconscious money beliefs shape your financial reality,and how to change them for abundance. My favorite book on the money subject.

**The Psychology of Money** – Morgan Housel

A beautifully written exploration of how emotion, ego, and behavior influence how we earn, save, and spend money.

**Rich Dad Poor Dad** – Robert Kiyosaki

A mindset-shifting classic about building financial independence, investing, and moving beyond the paycheck mentality.

# HEALTH & WELLNESS

**The New Menopause** – Mary Claire Haver, MD

A holistic and science-backed guide to navigating perimenopause and menopause with clarity, grace, and empowerment.

**Fast Like a Girl** – Dr. Mindy Pelz

Understand how to tailor fasting and nutrition to your hormonal cycle for better energy, mood, and long-term health.

# STAY IN TOUCH

Thank you for walking with us through The Power to Say Yes. We hope these pages have sparked new insights, opened fresh possibilities, and empowered you to embrace life more fully.
Our journey doesn't end here! We'd love to stay connected and continue supporting your growth:

- Join our community and mailing list. Scan the first QR code to sign up for updates, exclusive content, and invitations to online discussions. You'll be the first to hear about new resources and upcoming projects.

- Share your story. Your experiences matter. Scan the second QR code to tell us about your own "yes" moments, how this book has impacted you and the steps you're taking toward positive change. We're excited to feature select stories (with your permission) and celebrate your successes together.

- Reconnect in person. Throughout the year we host retreats and workshops designed to help you deepen these principles, connect with a like minded community, and create lasting transformation. Look out for announcements, and join us for an unforgettable experience.

Thank you again for being part of this journey. We can't wait to hear from you and to continue inspiring one another.